Castles & Painted Moments

ADULT COLORING BOOK WITH POETRY AND SELF-DISCOVERY

Aventuras De Viaje

Copyright SF Nonfiction Books © 2024

All Rights Reserved

No part of this document may be reproduced without written consent from the author.

www.SFNonfictionBooks.com

INTRODUCTION

Welcome to the enchanting realms where history blends with imagination, where the echoes of the past meet the brushstrokes of creativity. This isn't just a coloring book—it's a journey, a retreat, and a celebration of the timeless allure of castles and the painted moments they inspire.

Each page beckons you deeper into a landscape of majestic castles, ancient ruins, and breathtaking vistas, where stone walls and forgotten pathways become canvases of personal discovery. These scenes, symbols of endurance, romance, and the enduring narrative of history, await your colors to come alive. Coloring these moments offers not only a visual voyage but also a profound connection with the essence of these historic sanctuaries.

In the haste of our daily lives, finding time to pause and reflect is invaluable. This book invites you to slow down, to immerse yourself in a world of artistic detail and quiet contemplation, and to reconnect with the serene pulse of historical beauty. It's an opportunity to rekindle your imagination and fill it with the hues of antiquity and serenity.

Embark on this artistic journey, diving into the layers of castle architecture and the soothing act of coloring. Here, you're not merely observing the scenery; you're interacting with history, unleashing your creativity, and experiencing the peace of artistic mindfulness.

Discovering the Mosaic of Imagination

Dive deeper, and you'll find that this book has been meticulously crafted to enhance your personal journey:

- **Simple Activities:** Beyond just coloring, engage with activities designed to spark reflection and creativity. These gentle prompts will lead you to moments of introspection, serving as kindling for your inner fire.

- **Quotes:** Let the wisdom of personal development accompany you, illuminating your path as you add your own burst of color to the pages.

- **Positive Affirmations:** As you color, let these words of positivity uplift your spirit, molding your thoughts and inspiring a brighter perspective.

- **Poems and Haikus**: Delight in the poetic tales that complement the theme of this book, capturing life's varied rhythms and experiences. Each verse and every line serve as a muse for your artistic endeavors, enhancing your coloring journey with lyrical inspiration.

Embark on this coloring odyssey, immersing yourself in a world of diverse themes and the therapeutic embrace of art. Each page invites you on a unique journey, blending your creativity with the tranquility of coloring.

THANKS FOR YOUR PURCHASE

Get Your Next SF Nonfiction Book FREE!

Claim the book of your choice at:

www.SFNonfictionBooks.com/Free-Book

You will also be among the first to know of all the latest releases, discount offers, bonus content, and more.

Go to:

www.SFNonfictionBooks.com/Free-Book

Thanks again for your support.

Daily Blessing:
What made you smile today?

_____

_____

"Build your inner castle, one stone of courage at a time."

I am the architect of my own happiness.

Within these castle walls, I find
A quiet space, a peaceful mind.
I build my fortress strong and true,
A sanctuary just for you.

**Fortress of Solitude:
What did you do just for yourself today?**

_____

_____

"In the gardens of the mind, cultivate thoughts that bloom."

I build my life on a foundation of peace and self-acceptance.

Castle shadows fade,
Dawn whispers soft promises,
Day's canvas awaits.

Royal Decree:
What positive change will you initiate tomorrow?

_____

_____

"Every day is a new stone to fortify your resolve."

I am a seeker of beauty in everyday moments.

Above the castle, skies are wide,
With strokes of cloud that softly glide.
The colors blend at close of day,
Painting worries far away.

Castle Gardens:
What beauty did you notice around you?

_____

_____

"Let the tapestries of your life display your inner beauty."

I cherish the journey of self-discovery.

Hidden blooms in shade,
Secrets of a castle's heart,
Quiet beauty sings.

Royal Banquet:
What meal did you enjoy today,
and why was it special?

_____

_____

"Draw the bridges to your soul; let only the worthy enter."

I embrace the wisdom of my experiences.

In gardens old, where time stands still,
The flowers bloom with their own will.
In every petal, wisdom lies,
A tale of seasons, under skies.

Hidden Treasures:
What are you grateful for in your life today?

_____

_____

"Look out from the towers of your experiences and foresee possibilities."

I am a guardian of my own peace.

Stories etched in stone,
Echoes of a thousand years,
Whispered by the wind.

Chivalrous Acts:
What act of kindness did you perform or receive?

_____

_____

"In the corridors of your mind, hang portraits of peace."

I reflect on my day with gratitude.

The silent stones tell tales untold,
Of brave hearts warm and winters cold.
Each brick and mortar holds a story,
Of past lives wrapped in glory.

Castle Restoration:
What can you improve in your surroundings?

_____

_____

"Unlock the ancient gates of your heart with keys of kindness."

I paint my thoughts with colors of positivity.

In the quiet dusk,
Castle turrets touch the stars,
Night's gentle embrace.

Scribe's Entry:
Write a thank-you note to yourself.

_____

_____

"Your spirit is the lord of the castle; rule with gentle wisdom."

I hold the key to unlocking my full potential.

Water mirrors the soul's request,
In tranquil moments, find your rest.
The castle's moat, deep and wide,
Reflects the heart that dwells inside.

Minstrel's Melody:
What song uplifts your spirits?

_____

_____

"Moats of doubt surround us; build bridges of confidence."

I am a masterpiece of my own making.

Stone paths wind unseen,
Through the heart's hidden corners,
Journeying within.

Royal Progress:
What small victory did you achieve today?

_____

_____

"The highest tower offers the broadest view; elevate your mind."

I am in harmony with the melody
of my heart.

Echoes of yore in halls so grand,
Each stone a story, from distant land.
In these walls, history sleeps,
And in its silence, the castle keeps.

Crown Jewels:
What personal qualities do you treasure?

_____

_____

"A mindful ruler listens to the whispers of the land."

I explore the corridors of my mind with curiosity.

Castles under stars,
Night blankets the ancient stones,
Dreams whisper old tales.

Wizard's Wisdom:
What wise advice would you give yourself?

_____

_____

"Explore the mysterious rooms of your identity."

BEYOND THESE PAGES

A Deeper Dive into Art and Soul Awaits!

This book is but a chapter in a voyage where creativity meets depth.

Craving more? Explore the link below and weave deeper into the tapestry of art and emotion.

www.SFNonfictionBooks.com/Adult-Coloring-Books

A HEARTFELT THANK YOU

As the colors on these pages have come to life, so has our shared journey in this artistic realm. I am deeply grateful for your trust in choosing this book, and more so for allowing it to be a part of your self-care and personal journey.

Taking time for oneself is a gift—a silent promise of growth, introspection, and rejuvenation. By picking up the colors and filling these pages, you've not just created art but have also woven moments of peace, reflection, and creativity into your life.

Thank you for making space for yourself, for embracing the wonders within these pages, and for dancing to the rhythm of the lines and hues within this book. Your journey here is a testament to the beauty of dedicating time to one's soul and spirit.

If you enjoyed this journey and wish to explore more, know that there are other themes awaiting your artistic touch. Dive into new worlds and let your imagination flow.

From the deepest corner of my heart, thank you for bringing this book to life. Until our next artistic adventure together, cherish the colors of your journey and continue to shine.

Warmly,

Aventuras De Viaje

ABOUT THE AUTHOR

Aventuras has three passions: travel, writing, and learning new skills.

Combining these three things, Miss Viaje spends her time exploring the world and learning about anything and everything that interests her, from yoga, to music, to science, and more.

Aventuras takes what she discovers and shares it through her books.

www.SFNonfictionBooks.com

www.ingramcontent.com/pod-product-compliance
Lightning Source LLC
Chambersburg PA
CBHW081621100526
44590CB00021B/3541